On the North Slope

Brosman's vivid new poems display a radiant sense of reality. Whether she brings us to a Southwestern desert house, a Colorado mountaintop, or a Las Vegas casino, we feel truly transported there by her sharpness poetic eye and the quiet authority of her music. These are wise, worldly, and surprisingly tender poems.
—Dana Gioia

Brosman is eminent among American poets who still believe in the traditional verities of measure and making sense. Pleasures abound in this generous collection of shapely, musical, life-affirming poems.
— X. J. Kennedy

On the Northern Slopes testifies passionately to a long life richly lived. She provides vivid descriptions of the flora, fauna, and landscapes of regions she knows intimately. The exquisitely crafted formal and free verse poems on a panoply of themes from personal to universal show us why Brosman is one of the most accomplished and fully-rounded poets writing today. This is an extraordinary collection whose pleasures are not to be missed.
—Alexander Pepple, editor of *Able Muse* and *Able Muse Anthology,*
      administrator & founder of *Eratosphere*

Catharine Savage Brosman's scintillating verses are like seventeenty-century Dutch seascapes—supremely controlled yet compassionating observations of people and places loved and too often lost, seen against a wide, wild world full of beauty, movement and possibility. Every heartfelt but precise syllable of each poem reveals an expert practitioner of unusual musicality, warmth, intelligence, and culture

—Derek Turner, novelist and editor of the *Quarterly Review*

Brosman's *On the North Slope* comprises a dazzling selection of beautiful poems that take in the vast sweep and depth of the natural world; yet, to apply the term "nature poet" as a pejorative would be to miss how, with an exquisite eye for precise detail and an ear for music, Brosman is always framing and defining the human element within that natural context. Whether she is describing "the petioles of a flower, or the great blazing flank of a snow-covered mountainside," she is a master of "telluric words," of "the miniscule and the sublime."

—Rob Griffith, author of *The Moon from Every Window*

These finely chiselled poems enact a movement from an avowedly anecdotal delight in person, place, and nomenclature to a heightened sensitivity that allows the reader to share in unsuspected depths of feeling. *On the North Slope* is, above all, a celebration of the rich compatibility of the intellectual and affective realms.

—Michael Tilby, Selwyn College, Cambridge

On the North Slope

Poems

Catharine Savage Brosman

MERCER UNIVERSITY PRESS

MACON, GEORGIA

MERCER
UNIVERSITY PRESS

Endowed by
TOM WATSON BROWN
and
THE WATSON-BROWN FOUNDATION, INC.

To my husband, Patric Savage,
and my daughter, Katherine Brosman Deimling,
with love and appreciation to them both, always.

"Art does not reproduce the visible; it renders visible."
—Paul Klee, "Creative Confession" (1920),
quoted in G. di San Lazarro, *Klee*, p. 105.

MUP/P444

© 2012 Catharine Savage Brosman
Published by
Mercer University Press
1400 Coleman Avenue
Macon, Georgia 31207
All rights reserved

First Edition

Books published by Mercer University Press are printed on acid-free paper
that meets the requirements of American National Standard for Information
Sciences—Permanence of Paper for Printed Library Materials.

Mercer University Press is a member of Green Press Initiative
(greenpressinitiative.org), a nonprofit organization working to help
publishers and printers increase their use of recycled paper and decrease
their use of fiber derived from endangered forests. This book is printed on
recycled paper.

Brosman, Catharine Savage.
On the north slope : poems / Catharine Savage Brosman. -- 1st ed.
p. cm.
Includes bibliographical references.
ISBN 978-0-88146-273-9 (pbk. : alk. paper) -- ISBN 0-88146-273-X
(pbk. : alk. paper)
I. Title.
PS3552.R666O5 2012
811'.54--dc23
2011050538

Contents

Acknowledgments

Grateful acknowledgment is made to the publishers of the following magazines and anthologies, where the poems mentioned first appeared: *Able Muse:* "Agnes de Mille in Paris," "Alpenglow," "Anniversary," "Ars poetica," "Beaumarchais in the Tribunal," "Cerro Pedernal,""Edith's Party," "For a Close Friend Whose Father Hanged Himself," "For a Friend Whose Husband Died in the Madrid Airport," "Garlic," "On the Mesa Top," "Stockholm, June 2000"; *Alabama Literary Review:* "Blue Norther," "On the North Slope," "Winter Sunset, Pike's Peak"; *The Anglican:* "In an English Cathedral"; *Chronicles: A Magazine of American Culture:* "Cheese," "Colorado Winds," "Las Campanas"; *Classical Outlook:* "Amaryllis," "Iris"; *Concho River Review:* "Growing Pains"; *Evansville Review:* "An Evening at Eleanor's"; "For Friends of a Man Who Died in a Las Vegas Casino"; *First Things:* "At the Ballet," "Yellow-Crowned Night Heron"; *Humanitas* (an online magazine): "Carrots," "Florissant Fossil Beds," "In the Brooklyn Museum," "North Park"; *Jubilee Anthology:* "Blue Heron on Blue Sky"; *Measure:* "For One Whose Husband Drowned in the Backyard Pool," "Scarlet Gilia"; *Modern Age:* "Cabbage," "Four-O'Clocks"; *The Pennsylvania Review* (an on-line magazine): "On Seeing Patric Again"; *Quarterly Review:* "Eggs," "Snow Clouds," "Winter Light"; *Sewanee Review:* "Driftwood," "Liszt in Weimar"; *South Carolina Review:* "Evelyn," "Hibernia"; *Southern Humanities Review:* "Yeats and Maud Gonne, 1891"; *Town Creek Poetry* (an on-line magazine): "Kim Kum-sun," "Sarabande," "Themes for Piano and Poetry"; *Trinacria:* "Abed," "At the Art Show," "L'elisir d'amore" (under the title "The Elixir of Love"), "For a Late Cat (I)," "For a Late Cat (II)," "Honey."

Some of these poems appeared in my chapbook *Trees in a Park* (Thibodaux, LA: Chicory Bloom Press, ©2010); three of them, "Bluebonnets," "Scarlet Gilia," and "Tree in Winter," were republished in *Trinacria.* "Bluebonnets" and "Tree in Winter" were republished on the site of *Eratosphere*, a poetry blog.

Ars poetica*

In art I like verisimilitude—
not slavish imitation of the real,
but—even the extraordinary—viewed
for truth's increase and durable appeal.

The murderer may be portrayed, the fraud,
though less than monstrous: thus Medusa's snakes
need taming; tragic figures we applaud
must not seem more perverse than their mistakes.

Peculiarities and accidents
of landscape, person, fruit need not be changed,
yet profit from restraint and ornaments.
The tulip's streaks may well be rearranged,

as language purged of oaths and vulgar words,
save bits of flavoring: a phrase or so
reveals the man; we do not want the turds.
Since verities depend on what we know

already, hid in shadows of neglect,
the artist's light should rarely be extreme,
nor must his lens distort—instead, direct
uncommon focus to a common theme,

by vision, measured understanding, tact.
Depict, then, golden peach and worm; eschew
grotesque or alien creature, vicious act;
use artifice to complement what's true.

* Notes on this and other poems will be found at the end of the collection.

I: A Commonwealth of Place

Six Cold Poems from Colorado

1. On the North Slope

—For Patric

On the north slope, snow is obstinate, staying on (despite
pale sun and mild air during afternoon) in dense stands
of pines, behind boulders, shrubbery, and knolls—
rectangles, squares, curved patches, wedges, and half-moons—
white shadows, though themselves in shade.
The spruce wear open cloaks and hoods thrown back.
Snow lights the Rampart Range, of course, and also Zebulon's
great peak, both east- and western face, the dimple

copiously powdered and its tracery of clefts and ridges outlined
well. The range and hillsides facing south
are barren, though—dry, colorless. Seen from the air,
on the flight northward yesterday, brown winter fields,
plowed last year in patterns, reminded me of Braque and Gris—
monochromatic canvases of circles fitted
among squares. Here, too, the scene is almost cubist, with planes
of white in skewed arrangements. I'm on the north side

also—the darker face, quicker of shadow, moving into night—
with snow in my hair, but a heart's fire glowing.
I remember driving, in the year 2000, from Grand Junction
to Ouray, Durango, and Pagosa Springs, and then
into New Mexico, with snowbanks nearly all
the way, the pavement covered, and new snow falling—
nature taking back the road—and scarcely any other
car; and how, in Taos finally, I thanked the spirit of the peaks,

and stood in awe beside the great blue spruce, where crystals
of a final shower—melting as they hit my face—
remained, each one set off, a jewel on a velvet mantle.
The great joy of my winter waited for me, still
ahead some years. And then we met after long patience, many
miles. We've missed the drop-offs and endured
the drought; we've squared the circle. In summer, we'll gaze
out along the slope, green from its snow bath, signaling.

2. Winter Light

In mid-December, mackerel skies in banks
move swiftly, leaving patches of faint blue
and filtered rays of sun. The year outflanks
us, though we'd barely noticed. Its adieu,

as autumn blows itself away, is brief—
acknowledgment of passage, then a pause,
before the solstice turning brings relief.
One needs the wheel of seasons and their laws,

which temper and illuminate the range
of life. Fine mist along the river, rain,
raw wind out of the west befit our strange
hibernal mood of happiness and pain—

as winter light affords long, private hours
for thinkers, and for lovers growing old,
whose colloquies among late-blooming flowers
assay the keenest meanings of the cold.

3. Snow Clouds

—For Timothy Murphy

Pike's Peak was clear at dawn, with just a crown
of vapor on its noggin. A platoon
of snow clouds mars its face now, though—a frown
foretelling an assault by afternoon.

Along the breastworks of the Rampart Range,
they glower, bracing, gathering their wrath,
before they burst, and fire (as a change
from bombast) crystal manna in their path.

Odd light, a bit of goose-down blowing by,
wind rushing, then…bombardment! Snow is hurled
in volleys, stinging, melting in the eye
—frail, watery concoction of the world,

its ingenuity in every flake,
quite weightless, yet in quantity, a feat,
whose burden on the thirsty land will break
the drought, and nourish grass and winter wheat.

4. Tree in Winter

In frozen gestures—sculpted, fixed in place—
the maple tree, now leafless, stark, and blind,
devises, from its denudation, grace,
its seven limbs uplifted, arched, entwined;

like Shiva, who destroys and then creates—
the master of the universal dance,
a constant tourbillon, the round of fates,
disposing newly of the stuff of chance.

The tree's deep being orders the design
of root and trunk—no alien intent—
well replicated in each texture, line,
and leaf, implicit as the branch is bent.

And thus, in its intensity of fact,
it carries promise—sap run, dress of green—
its visions wedded in the verdant act
of opening its eye-buds, proud, serene.

5. Winter Sunset, Pike's Peak

There's fire to the west, around the peak
and stretching northward; it's Old Sol again,
a-lolling on his daybed. He'd been weak
at noon and let the clouds prevail, but then

aroused, as if ashamed. A scarlet streak
shoots upward from the embers in a glen,
and in an aureole of green—a freak—
two birds pass, dark—a crow, a canyon wren;

while remnants of the overcast disguise
themselves as smoke, and shadowed snow that lies
along the mountain's clefts and shelves looks ashen,

—deep cold transformed in the beholder's eyes
to everything a fire signifies:
hearts frozen, then awakening to passion.

6. Colorado Winds

Like undergraduates all partied out but anxious,
after some hours, to start anew, great winds,
having blown themselves to bits a day or so
ago, threw up their hands last night,
either at our sleep or their own indolence, and roused
again. They came from the cardinal points,
at least three. Rowdy and boastful, roaring
as though drunk, they lay siege to the maple trees—

no leafy ornaments to rattle there, however—
and assaulted the blue spruce, sturdy and resistant
to attacks, but fitting instruments
for moan and whine and whistle. Gusts—and even
gales—and whirlwinds sported madly
through the darkness; clouds, as if pursued, scuttled
on across the moon. It was all dry antics,
wild shenanigans lacking sense or beauty,

but carried out, you might say, according to academic
formula (ominous sky, branches shaken,
sundry brittle twigs, sand, bits of trash hurled
against the windowpanes). Is this the last word
of the winter, a playful cry, a bang?
Certainly not; snows will ride across Ute Pass again
in March, then reappear in April, maybe
May, in springtime form—heavy crystal flakes,

rhinestones for a hat or a lapel. I must not mind
greatly; this is just the turbulence of the Front Range,
which catches weather, wet or dry, swirls,
beats, or cuts it up as by a Cuisinart,
then redistributes it, a little carelessly. Better
than the Caribbean or the Gulf, with their hurricanes;
at least we won't get flooded out, unlike New Orleans
when that evil eye approaches, carrying

days' worth of rainfall and whipping the tidal lakes
and bayous back across the wetlands—
next, the city and its canals, soon swallowed
by the sea. Let the battering continue. I'll take refuge
in my mind, still Katrina-shaken but no longer
soaked like soggy bread, incapable of thought—nor
a sieve, admitting waves of dismay. I'll play
the winds like memories—innocuous bluster, dark *frissons.*

High Plains

In late June heat, we're crossing, Pat and I, through Texas,
heading to the Panhandle and the High Plains—Lubbock,
Amarillo, Dalhart, Texline. Cattle, oil and gas,
soybeans, cotton, corn for food and fodder, truck farms:
what wealth is here to meet our needs! To the north,
the Oklahoma Panhandle, Kansas, then Nebraska
and the two Dakotas, where my friend Tim Murphy crafts
his poems and plants wheat—the very image

of true, classic culture, Virgil's *Georgics* in the modern
mode.—*Heat*, I said, and solstice-brilliant sun,
tenacious. And the wind. "What's to stop it from blowing
from any direction?" Yet the world's work here
goes on—combines in the fields, pump jacks bending,
drilling rigs and maintenance crews around the wells,
pickups shuttling on the highway, business carried on
in the courthouse, and a few old men, lean still,

their faces rutted, chewing the fat. We've got
the Canadian River behind us now, and we're dropping off
the Caprock, which, friable, breaks into many draws
and canyons: it's green waterfall around us, something
like Niagara in earth. The descent is not, however,
into an inferno, since we rise again, still higher, and—day
growing long in the tooth—we've got breeze and shadows
on the road. Thunderheads already have built up,

high bastions full of ammunition, glowering.
What a lordly progress, this, and such distinctive land,
with its own rationale, not needing others. Lightning
smoulders to the west, then leaps. We've reached
the grasslands at the very top of Texas and New Mexico,
and rain arrives with us—drops the size of a half-dollar,
splashing in the soil, making windshield mud.
It's time to stop now anyway. We're greeted by the scent

of ozone-freshened rain on soil and in the air, and trees—
pines, cottonwoods, even blue spruce—showered,
then showering on us. Tomorrow, early, we will glimpse
the Sangre de Cristos—red at dawn, in afternoon
blue revery—and then the Front Range, crowning the plain,
its peaks bejeweled by snow. We do not compromise:
no paper fortunes, no fool's gold—only a commonwealth
of place, vast *llanos*, vaster light, high truths writ in earth.

North Park

Among tall aspen—leafy, elegant—and spruce, severe,
the road has crested over Willow Creek Pass,
leading from Grand County and the enormous basin-land
called Middle Park into its smaller kin,
North Park. It's neat, as if an architect had laid it out,
with mountains on all sides, framing well
the smooth green stretch of boreal leys. Cattle
animate the scene, some grazing, heads pointed downwind,

others moving single-file, to water, or on some whimsy
of their own. Streams meander here and there, marked
by cottonwoods or willows. Elsewhere, hay
lies in fresh bales or has been stacked already.
A few low spots are alkaline—white or discolored
crystal stuff. The world is well away.
The rustic, unpretentious town where we have lunch
is Walden; and Thoreau, if he were here, would recognize

a kindred spirit, though he might go even farther, settling
by a pond where bison wallow. We too like
the isolation and the vast perspectives, ending only
at blue skylines; and my love—still young—
for you ripples and besports itself in the shimmering light
across the fields, all green and yellow. Yet
I do not love you less in crowds, in dark remembrances
or cramping of the mind, the moments when a curtain

→

falls across reflection, or the ashen sky weighs heavily.
That is the proof—joy together in this mountain
summer, brilliant even as it wanes, and also in what follows,
necessarily: in North Park, winds bearing down
from the plains and ranges of Wyoming, cold entrenched
(I shiver at the thought), and, for us,
pinched-in winter days, city traffic and routines,
but high ground of the heart, high love, holding us up.

Alpenglow

The dawn was ominous: the rising sun,
competing with dark clouds, rain-laden, low,
skipped out —a feeble player, shining done.
But earlier we'd been touched by alpenglow,

a scene for the matutinal, with red
illumination on the western range—
not sanguinary: royal purple, spread
before the sunrise in a strange

anticipation—brilliant overture
to daylight, or the postlude to a dream.
It painted valleys, drew the crests with sure,
contrasting outlines, magnified the gleam

of glaciers—vision, brief phenomenon
that matches our impermanence. A thought
of fire is kindled. Soon enough, new dawn.
In what a round of changes are we caught,

with little time left, but the wit and grace
of passion! Great Orion with his bow
and arrow walks the heavens. We shall race
tonight in love, then rise for alpenglow.

Florissant Fossil Beds

The sun has warmed us through the thin, high mountain
air, and, panting a bit, we hasten to find shade
in ponderosa pine and spruce before continuing
along the sunlit path that winds among the fossil beds
of Florissant. We've admired the fallen giants'
huge remains—Eocene sequoias turned
to stone, the limbs long gone but the bases still upright,
petrified after tides of volcanic fire and ash

roiled across the valley, more than thirty million years
ago. There are signs here, too, of paleo-Indians,
mixed with artifacts of Uncompaghre Utes and Apaches
of the Jicarilla tribe, who left their potsherds
scattered in the redwood ruins; too, abundant shale,
imprinted with the brittle, delicate debris of ages
even earlier—times I cannot imagine—
when sediments, compressed, solidified, took hostages—

living witnesses from sea and earth. Remnants hide still
among alpine flowers of late August, nearly
unnoticed, and so ephemeral that, by this evening,
many will have dropped or withered.—Surely, then,
we must feel closer bonds to them than to the seeds, fruit,
leaves, and animals of aeons before ours;
yet these frail butterflies in stone, these spiders, bees
like fetuses, these flowers, pollens, ostracods

compressed in shale are eerily familiar, as if—though
not created then—we also might have been there,
in promise as moist bits of protoplasm—a great thought
of the planet come to light much later, like seeds
in volcanic paste, infertile, but whose distant
kindred live now on these slopes—leafy maple,
densely-fronded fir, sharing in immense
commotions—time, while unseemly, tying us together.

On the Mesa Top

Here we are atop the vast, imposing mesa
called the "Monument"—a monument to nature, certainly.
It's really a huge canyon complex, cut out
by the ages through stone layers, notched and denticled,
with monoliths standing alone, tragic figures
left when other actors and some scenery were blown
away. Getting here takes time, on shelf roads,
serpentine and steep. But what a vista! Book Cliffs,

whitewashed in the light, stretch out northwest;
eastward, the Grand Mesa breaks, a massive tidal wave
unfurling into troughs and plains. We've found a table
for our lunch, within a circle of red cedar
and fine Utah juniper, with twisted trunks and berries, blue,
so plentiful that vats of gin could be produced
from just one tree. So we get out cool water
and the leftovers from last night's dinner. The air

is dry, the blue as if distilled, the sunlight brilliant
through dense whorls of leaves and louvered
limbs. Suddenly, a swishing sound, and fluttering: a bird
dives past my shoulder, drops, and settles
on the table edge before us. He's been here before;
he knows there's food, and dares to trust us. He's
a Colorado jay, just slightly crested, azure as a shadowy
distant mountain. His feet are delicate but long,

prehensile; the legs are tiny stilts. We stare, not moving,
watching him watch us. He wings off to a tree
just opposite, rejoins (we think) his mate, imparts
some matters. She also, then, swoops down
and lands, looking interrogative. When she in turn flies
back into the thicket, I take out a roll, part-eaten,
tear it, place the pieces where the birds'
sweet presence left a rustling after them. No further

invitation is required. Here he is: a gust, a glide, a swerve,
and half the bread is carried off. Shortly,
she arrives and takes the rest. What ease, yet what
commotion as they gather in the weathered heart
of juniper! It remains for us—birds in the wilderness
and kin—to feel their hidden being, celebrate
their passage, know this moment on the immemorial
rock, leaving behind no crumbs, but thoughts, thoughts.

Driftwood

—In memory of
Edward C. Hill, M.D.

The bridegroom from Ohio and his bride
arrived in Colorado, penniless,
and settled in the mountains to the west
of Denver, where he hoped to pan for gold
or stake a claim. Amanda's family
was prosperous, but she had been denounced
and disinherited, because the man
she chose as husband was (or seemed to be)

a ne'er-do-well; her sister, who remained
in favor, would inherit all.—They lived,
poor hermits, in a tent; the husband, weak
perhaps already, suffered from the cold,
fell ill, coughed blood, and could no longer work.
Although a foothills doctor visited
(Amanda, swallowing her pride, had fetched
him, owning that she could not pay withal)

there was no remedy, in fact. The hand
of fate sketched out the sign of death,
but waited. What few dollars they had saved
were drained away; and then a child was born,
nursed meagerly, as all Amanda's strength
was drawn for it. The doctor often came,
and from his own resources gave them food,
wool blankets, medicine. Tubercular

but obstinate, the man resolved to live
despite his lesioned lungs: a man is held
in hostage to his love, his sacrifice,
and others' earlier. The child died first,
the smaller prize; the father followed.—Time,
a joker, whether gay or somber, looks
for moments when its tricks will be received
with wry appreciation of their irony

and, often, bitter rue. While angry still,
Amanda's parents had not long endured
estrangement; then the sister, although young,
was seized by some strange malady, and she
in turn was dead. The family fortune fell
to her who had been cursed and sent away.
Informed, she traveled to Ohio, sold
the house and other property, and bade

farewell. She shipped the antique furniture
—invaluable driftwood from her past—
by the Ohio to St. Louis, then
out west. A wealthy woman now, she left
the mountains and their lode—two modest graves—
for Denver, where she led a widow's life,
quite proper, in a handsome house, alone
except for phantoms in her memory

and friends. She did not wed, for what was lost
would not be found again. The doctor too
had settled there and married; he became
well-known, esteemed. In time, remembering
that charity had never been repaid,
she left him everything—fine furnishings
and silver, monogrammed, good real estate—
a bid to snatch late meaning from the stars.

Horizon

—For Nancy McCahren; for Pat, also
—July, 2007

Driving down from Colorado, via Questa
and Arroyo Hondo, toward Taos, we are drawn
as if by magnetism into vast perspectives—
pale sagebrush plateau, Sangre de Cristo range—
all so beautiful it's almost painful to the mind.
This is the prospect Lawrence thought
the loveliest on earth. The horizon pulls
us on all sides—even its retreating angles,

changing in the curves; ahead, the landscape
paints itself in rising contours, planes,
floating up to Wheeler Peak. We're like girls
again, traveling together as we did in Europe,
fifty years ago. The light is brilliant,
as in Greece, blanching out the desert sea,
which waves and laps at leafy islands—
poplars, cottonwoods, blue spruce. We follow

the Paseo narrows into town between huge trees,
aligned as if in recognition of us. Nothing solemn
will attend this visit, though; we do not tread,
but glide along, as it were, in the blue air,
anticipating plenitude, taking freedom
as a falcon rides the currents. So I look out
now from the balcony of our hotel and gaze
upward to the crest of the sierra, deep green,

shading into dark, against skies of aquamarine,
fleeced by white sails. What is that presence
in the air, a beckoning, as if a spirit
moved at the day's edge? The wind rustles
venerable cottonwoods, and scudding clouds
pass above the peak; but there is something more,
a feeling that the future is afoot. We breathe
it in, the sense of possibility, of ripeness,

though it's still July. And, over drinks, Nancy
asks me about Pat. Strange foreshadowing:
when we return to Colorado, there's a message
from him, out of the distant blue, after
forty years—turning the past inside out,
the dark core of memory become a new horizon,
blue-rippling, bright with amber sun,
ourselves again there walking, finally, together.

Las Campanas

From the patio, we look out westward on the mesa—
native flowers, piñon, cedar, juniper, a bit
of sage—toward the Jemez Mountains, turning purple
as the sun canters down. It's *Las Campanas*,
near a small bell tower, west of Santa Fé.
There's lovely quiet here—the campanile
is, I think, emblematic only, and the cathedral bells
are not heard so far from town; but something in the air

reminds one that this place is sonorous, its echo
reaching from days of native chants and Fray Oñate,
through Archbishop Lamy and the words
of Willa Cather, to this evening, with the playful wind
carilloning through the brush. The moon
is rising now behind us, full, sounding its bright gong
above the Sangre de Cristo range, illuminated
like a rood screen by the setting sun across the sky,

which radiates in ruddy gold, a monstrance. Little clouds,
tinctured red, row swiftly by, a dry regatta. So
we turn and gaze from one world to another,
embraced by dark blood on the eastern mountains
and the moon—and, to the west, the mesa,
with its solar drama. The gods are sporting,
also. Beams of sun, crisscrossed by clouds, design
a giant tennis racket, and the moon, a ball lobbed high

and lifted past the backdrop, hangs thirty degrees
or so above the earth, and in this altitude
just won't come down.—We are ourselves, not
others, but we also are the past, and thus are multiple—
bright bells, ringing with the tones
that sounded through this land for those who loved it.
Over the Jemez, rain begins to fall, a scrim,
veiling red cloud; the great game goes on to another set.

Cerro Pedernal

Northwest of Española, past the town of Abiquiu—
a hamlet, rather—where O'Keeffe had a house,
and painted—past Ghost Ranch, with its persistent spirit—
we turn off to the west, through the north flank
of the Jemez Mountains. We've seen the red and yellow
cliffs she stylized, the dark green foliage
on her mesas—piñon, cedar, juniper—the blue, pale
water-hue, of her skies, black lava badlands, noon's

white cowl. —All familiar, all intense—and chilling,
in its lovely, visceral transcendence. Now,
as the road bends, I recognize the Cerro Pedernal—
Flint Hill—really a narrow ridge, but, from our vantage
point, round and castellated, then, as we progress,
a ship's high prow above the undulating desert. So—
though wind erodes it more each century—
the prehistoric dwellers saw it and ascended it, finding

flint for tools, studying the heavens day and night,
admiring distant peaks, looking for signs.
As we approach, I scale it in my mind: Mesa Escoba first,
and its basalt, then the taluses and shoulders
of the Pedernal, the battlements, the caprock at the top;
I think of Georgia's ashes there, among the stones.
What space the eye possesses here!—drawing
toward us hills and outcrops, deep arroyos, evidence

of earth's imaginative turmoil, water, fire, wind—
everything that we are not, but need and love and take
for ours. We're turning now, seeing the Pedernal
as one long tailing. Ahead, high painted bluffs
bleed color onto the horizon, evening yellow, crimson,
grey, a canvas almost pointillist, yet bold—
as we bleed in our acts, life running out in stripes
and bruises, leaving traces, brilliant genii, in the dust.

At the Circle A Ranch

We're seated, after dinner, on the well-worn terrace—
broken flagstones, roots pushing up, steps
leaning. Venerable oaks, ponderosa (fronds like fans),
spruce, and a huge apricot tree canopy the lodge,
veranda, and the Sun Room, where we'll sleep
tonight, two blankets over us. Facing us, in a grassy
park, three small stands of tall and supple
aspen, planted in the sixties, catch the slanted

mountain sunlight in their leafy nets and iterate
by whispers everything the wind has said.
Farther down, a sour-apple orchard and two meadows
meet the forest, where a path, nearly invisible,
led me earlier to the headstone of a former owner,
buried on the land she loved. Beyond, I found
a priestly piñon pine of great girth, spread, loftiness—
five hundred years in age, still freshening that age

with new twigs and needles. We might have stayed
in the town of Cuba, some five miles away;
but those motels, or tourist courts, were said to be
(and looked) not only old, but dubious. Instead,
we've got rustic simplicity, clean beds and towels,
and, as a sitting room, a lounge displaying
hides, paws, heads, and racks of game—cougar, elk—
hunted in the forties. —How hard it was then,

when my parents undertook to civilize me! All
I wanted could have fit onto that summer property
of Grandmother's, west of Kenosha Pass—
cabin, porch, iron stove, daybed; a creek; rounded
stones and boulders from a glacial till; lodgepole, piñon,
ponderosa pine, fir and aspen, needles underfoot;
books, an old Victrola; hours as if suspended,
and the world well away: Arcadia, both pastoral

and wild—the very workshop of the flute and lyre,
but nearly solitary. Ah, the world! In due course
I acquired manners, met conditions others
would impose, and tasted love. The winds of age
have blown me back. Late susurration in the branches
answers these reflections; birds take wing
and swoop as if by rite, then settle, while we cultivate
accord—full harmonies, deep resonance, telluric words.

Three for Patric's Eightieth

1. Hibernia

So here we are in the town of Swords—Fingal,
County Dublin. "You can walk
through Dublin, but you must run through Swords,
because it's full of Savages." Tonight
we'll celebrate the eightieth anniversary
of Patric's birth, with a fine *ceilidh* organized

by J.C. and Geraldine: first, dinner for eighteen,
all family; then eight more to come
for drink and song with us. The weather's
cool and damp, with rain one day in Howth
and Malahide, where we had lunch,
and mist swirling around the Eye of Ireland;

still, we've driven into Dublin, marveled
at the Spire, visited the General Post Office,
meditated on the Easter Rising; and we've toured
the Wicklow Mountains, admired
the manly slopes, looked down on the county
where a fifth of Ireland lives. Off the main road,

we visited the Deutschen Soldatenfriedhof—
a cliff that drips with flowers and greenery, a stele,
and stone crosses marking graves
of Luftwaffe aviators who, off course,
crashed nearby. Then Glendalough, its two lakes
stained by peat, the color of strong tea,

their glaze reflecting autumn browns and reds
from kneeling hillsides. A rainbow
arced above the lough. I thought of your father,
leaving his isle before the Great War.
Ah, Ireland! Bleeding so much, suffering long
the ulcers of occupation, draining away.

2: Caledonia

Since I'm part Scots-Irish, this too is an ancestral
home, that of the Elliotts. We're here,
though, not for family visits but for learning—
a little bit of mine to be spread around
a university. First, though, touring, on a pleasant
Scottish Sunday. We're taken by our host,

truly a gentleman, along the braes of Loch Lomond
for morning coffee at Cameron House
and a viewing of Ben Lomond, across
the water—a capricious majesty,
visible at moments, eclipsing then in cloud. Little
whitecaps form, and by turns the lake is blue

and iron-gray. In the car again, we run northward
near the shore—gaining altitude, twisting
in a leafy half-light, finally emerging
by the shore, with sheep on both sides. I return
the gaze of peaks with snowy shoulders,
"stern and wild." Next, it's lunch at "Bonnie Braes,"

then back to "home," a fire, friends, white wine,
a haggis dinner. Beside such graciousness,
what I'll provide is modest. Strange,
though: something in my talk the following day
annoys the resident post-colonialist.
Later, at the restaurant, he interrogates and baits

me, attacks my politics, presses wine on me, tries
to get me drunk. ("The School will pay.")
Our host and hostess are appalled, embarrassed.
Scotland's reputation will not suffer
in our eyes, however: it is plain the man's a fool,
conceited, and in the bargain an Oxonian.

3: Britannia

From Bridge of Allan it requires four trains to get
to Sheffield, where we'll see friends
from '96. And Pat does well, hoisting himself
and his case into the carriage, helping
me, enduring a beastly wind on the platform
while we wait at Doncaster, and a noisy,

jostling crush of England's youth, free for half-
term, journeying to Manchester airport. Sheffield
is dark when we arrive but milder
than expected, with only gentle rain. Our room
looks out on Victoria Quays and a small
marina, oddly picturesque. A nap, and then

we toast our happiness and others'. Next day,
it's a tour to Derwent Reservoir,
where pilots of the RAF did practice runs, nearly
at the water's surface, learning to fly
below the radar. Then, we're on to Leicestershire,
another land of roots. My poor husband!

Have the old, however, gotten younger? Once,
octogenarians would sit and rock,
or tend their roses, and deplore their rheumatism.
Now we manage distant cities, days of travel,
running from one dinner to another.
Such hospitality—an en-suite room at the house

of friends, a lovely lunch in Cambridgeshire, a visit
to King's College Chapel, drives, a concert
at Leamington Spa—gives a bath of youth
as well as love. We shall carry on
to London and survive King's Cross, the football
fans, Heathrow—and salute our forefathers, our own.

II: Order under the Sun

Amaryllis

—For Patric

Such gorgeous flowers, such a classic name—
evoking Virgil and Theocritus,
a shepherdess of literary fame,
bucolic scenes, authentic, amorous.

They bloom late in a Colorado mode,
enjoying waning sunshine, altitude,
cool rains, the range of nature's earthy code,
expressive of my Rocky Mountain mood.

Six petals, broad, spread outward, curving down
form parasols of purple, crimson, gold;
long filaments, full anthers in a crown
entice fat bees into the sepals' fold,

and butterflies, who hover, dive, then rise
on dusty wings unfolded for their flight.
Daylilies flourish also—no surprise—
and belladonna lilies, a delight

of nomenclature, pointing to desire—
to deadly nightshade, too, that toxic weed,
la belle dame sans merci, whose inner fire
can calm, or cure, or kill, like beauty's seed.

Thus gardens can be fatal, still—their grace
misleading us, since good is evil's twin,
and vice, resenting features of its face,
demands respect—fair homage paid to kin.

→

A lively toad goes scampering in the leaves.
Each amaryllis shakes its pollened head,
as afternoon declines and summer grieves.
We also to the growing dark are wed.

Honey

Mellifluous—it's such a lustrous word!
—suggesting fluid flavor, liquid light,
the clear, melodic trilling of a bird,
a mellow, sweet appeal to appetite.

Within the honey's amber heart, late rays
of sunset, captive, illustrate their glow,
with insects' industry on summer days
preserved and concentrated in its flow.

Whatever feeds the bees' transforming powers—
alfalfa, clover, cat-claw, mellilot,
palmetto, orange, or the rarest flowers—
is changed to pleasure in the honey pot.

Now, worker bees are withering in the hive,
while we endure, apparently preferred,
and, in our greater scope of living, thrive—
economy of nature, or absurd?

The essence of this apian husbandry,
although ephemeral, gives evidence,
at least, that meaning goes beyond the bee,
a providential legacy—art's sense.

Blue Heron on Blue Sky

Wings wide, majestic in its upward arc,
a heron animates the evening sky—
twice blue by its device—then draws the park
in leafy waves to meet the moving eye.

Inflected toward its nest, I think—a pine
or cypress near the bayou bank—it turns
downstream, then circles, disappears. A fine
commotion, lingering a moment, burns

on blue—by white-hot iron—an absence. Words
remain suspended also, but a trace
of flight becomes us: lovers, homing birds,
again as one in wing-beat and embrace.

Iris

How multivalent!— great prismatic arc
connecting distant corners of the skies,
or leaping over treetops in a park;
marine enchantment mirrored by green eyes;

and *Iridaceae*, resplendent blooms—
blue, violet, white, and yellow on parade—
whose petals—velvet, ruffled, bearded plumes—
suggest a rainbow for a dryads' glade.

The basal leaves, tough, pointed, straight as knives,
protect their other selves—a flowered cache—
enjoying thus, vicariously, lives
made beautiful in color and panache.

Blue flags, which flourish in the mountain air,
adorn my mind's nostalgic garden; phlox,
petunias, columbine, and maidenhair
fill out the scene, dispersed among the rocks,

where I collect my memories, and muse—
till Iris, messenger to gods, appears,
diaphanous in spectral veils, with news
of love, and scatters light and souvenirs,

which tie together past and present time—
bright garden of desire, sun streaked with rain,
your eyes again in mine—a paradigm
of final triumph in the heart's campaign.

Garlic

Allowing that it should not be advised
for lovers, still the *philosophe* Voltaire,
aware of vampires' weakness, duly prized
this pungent bulb, a versatile affair.

In fact, he knew that vampires were a myth;
disease was not, however, nor was death.
Abroad, one must take measures. Armed forthwith—
sachets of garlic at the throat, and breath

prepared (strong spices, onion, garlic, leek)—
a man might venture through the streets and feel
the better for his misanthropic reek,
a boon for him and for the commonweal.

The stench should keep them all at bay—the lout,
the nobleman, a chambermaid, His Grace;
if someone with the pox must hang about,
a foul effluvium assaults his face.

—With basil, onions, shallots, leeks, and chives,
today I found fresh garlic in the park
(a farmers' market). We lead different lives—
the latest denizens of Darwin's ark,

by which we have survived. No vampires here;
pox does not walk the streets. But now it's thought
that garlic trumps cholesterol, the fear
of overfed Americans; we ought

to eat it, drink the juice, take garlic pills.
I'll use it for potatoes, beans, French bread,
for pasta sauce, *ragoût*; our modern ills
must yield to proven means, or we'll be dead.

Cottonwood

—Santa Fé

With huge circumference, Cycloptic node,
and bark incised in heavy grooves by time,
it elegantly honors Canyon Road,
embodying arboreal sublime.

Out of a giant bough, like living stone,
a dancer forms, the spirit of the earth,
her body shaping as from Adam's bone,
limbs reaching upward toward a leafy berth.

The dance is virtual, its motion stilled
forever by the prison of the tree,
yet fluid, multiple, and as if willed
to stir, and set its nascent gestures free.

In sudden wind that tosses every leaf,
from solid wood a style seems to emerge,
the branches twisting, offering both grief
and gladness in choreographic urge.

A *pas*, an arabesque, a pirouette—
thus loveliness, implicit, is released,
acknowledging great immaterial debt,
until the windy harmonies have ceased.

Cabbage

It's homely, or considered so, because
resistant, humble, easy to conserve;
its perfume certainly gets no applause—
in short, a vegetable with little verve.

The name can signify good food (corned beef)—
but certain notions I could do without:
thin soups for prisoners, and poor relief;
bad cole slaw; wartime use of German *Kraut*;

the tale that children come from cabbage plants;
torn leaves that rot by the greengrocer's stall.
No matter. *Chou* means varied things in France:
plain *caulis* and its kindred, first of all—

then, joined to other words, a curious mix:
a flop; a worthless journalistic sheet;
inane or *simple-minded; in a fix;*
retire to the countryside, my sweet;

and *cream-puff,* finally. What fancy fare
appears so metaphoric? Not morels,
nor white asparagus, ripe Anjou pear,
real Russian caviare, snails in their shells.

Like apples, cabbages are almost myth,
suggesting something fundamental, true—
beneath life's incidental ornaments, its pith
and quintessential being, old and new.

→

To scorn a veggie, therefore, is unfair:
though given a fiery heart, a poet's mind,
we also are composed of water, air,
and earth—plain light and minerals, refined.

Humility can never be amiss,
nor love for cabbage in its leafy robe,
its head too hard to fathom the abyss
beyond the edges of our glorious globe.

Yellow-Crowned Night Heron

He's not alone—blue herons like to feed
here, egrets, mallards, ducks of lesser fame;
but his is an especially fine breed—
bold head with yellow crown, a stately name.

He stalks by night—and, happily for us,
at twilight too—along the bayou's verge,
immobile nearly, fishing without fuss,
obedient to nature's constant urge.

We call him "Our Bird," though he's wild and free,
indifferent to our admiring gaze,
his being wholly bound in what we see,
beyond the reach of reprimand or praise.

Four-O'Clocks

Such charming names: what would Linnaeus think,
taxonomist supreme?—*Anemone*,
pure Greek, might pass, but what of *knotweed, pink,*
jack-in-the-pulpit, bleeding heart, sweet pea,

or *black-eyed Susan, harebells, trumpet vine,*
snapdragon, bachelor's button, hollyhocks,
sweet William, Indian blanket, columbine,
broom, wolfbane, buttercups, and *four-o'clocks?*

This homeliness of nomenclature trumps,
in memory, at least, the learnèd terms—
as gardeners attend to compost, clumps
of sod, brick borders, weeds, manure, and worms

(the ground and company of floral art),
referring loveliness to other days
and leaving Latin, as the finer part,
to botanists. The ordinary ways

suffice to bear and honor sentiment—
an average wine, an inexpensive glass,
their poetry concealed in the intent.
Thus I remember pungent scents of grass,

and four-o'clocks, plebeian plants, beside
the house, half-wild. My father was not well,
but often watered them—a point of pride,
perhaps, for fortune's hostage; one could tell

how afternoon was waning when the furled
buds opened into little parasols,
quick to display their mauve or rose-hued world
and quick to drop and die. Such fate befalls

whole gardens, gone, with their quotidian
familiars—foxglove, larkspur, baby's breath—
a destiny decreed under the sun
to erudite and plain, by *mors* and death.

Eggs

These handy little embryos, compact
and versatile, though in a fragile shell,
propose both possibility and fact:
a sterile destiny—a bagatelle

for Nature—but a future in cuisine.
Consider sponge cake, custard, omelette,
eggs Benedict, raw eggs in milk (obscene),
meringue, sliced hard-boiled eggs with vinaigrette,

sauce *hollandaise*, rich icing, and eggs fried
or scrambled; you will see why a gourmet
does not disdain the modest foeticide
required for such dishes, plus soufflé,

frittata, quiche. That eye, though, looking out
accusingly at me recalls the sun
decapitated in its daily rout,
a virgin sacrificed, a god undone;

and as I whip the albumen and yolk—
at first translucent, then a golden froth—
I think that death must be a cosmic joke,
the deed of a dyspeptic Shiva, wroth

against the planet. Others may not care—
they'll eat a soft-boiled egg without a thought;
I picture nascent feathers in my hair,
and feel the chick's potential, come to naught.

Aviary

As if this were a wild preserve, what birds
collect here!—raptors, songbirds, waterfowl,
adapting well to urban circumstance,
proposing, by cohabitation, peace
and images of feathered nonchalance.
Yet this is Houston, sprawling megatown.
A hawk, his wings flanged wide, devises arcs,
a holding pattern of his own design;

five cattle egrets flush out, scattering
like rice thrown at a wedding, shuttle south,
pause briefly, then return, their errands done.
On pylons, sunlit pigeons lounge beside
six lanes of traffic; swifts by scores at dusk
collect in clouds, then line up on the wires—
good children, but still restless, changing place
to evening's music. In our oaks and pines,

we have an aviary—finches, doves,
a pair of cardinals, brown sparrows, jays,
and, waterside, on Bray's Bayou, black ducks,
who perch on rocks, and herons—one great blue,
two white—who favor shallows, where they stand
or stride with ballroom steps, deliberate—
long necks extended, eager eyes, poised beaks—
or suddenly take wing with strong, slow beats,

→

plane briefly, then alight just feet away
with plumage spread to brake, reminding me
of landing flaps. How can a simple bird
assume such density, eschewing drums—
no drama, cheering, advertising? Noise
is now the touchstone, the *sine qua non*
of most success. Nor will I mention size—
the be-all, end-all of our world, it seems—

nor other benchmarks. As the city longs,
a feverish patient, for pale light, fresh air,
and cooling linen on its brow, the birds
flock, chattering but orderly, or stalk
the current for a final meal, or soar,
and leave illuminations—quickening flash
of wing, idea in flight, trajectory,
serene, toward airy being and its shade.

Scarlet Gilia

Slim trumpets blowing, flaring into stars
(vermillion, speckled), strung on slender stems,
bright scarlet gilia offer avatars,
however small, of ideal beauty, gems

for steppe and mountain slope, delighting eyes
and thought. My grandfather collected things—
stones, plants and blossoms, butterflies—
and sorted them, displaying azure wings

on velvet under glass, wild flowers, dried
in albums, shadowed by their leaves, and rocks
in wooden cases, labeled, classified.
He favored scarlet gilia, harebells, phlox,

and other western flowers, but also kept
fine specimens from travels. Evidence
of all that enterprise is gone, except
cracked pages, crumbling stalks—and sentiments,

as I recall him, once, an old man, turned
to view a patch of gilia and admire
its fragile loveliness—and how he burned
(I think) to fill his lungs with young men's fire.

Cheese

A present from a god (great Bacchus, Pan,
Aristaeus, perhaps), and both a sign
and sustenance of cultivated man,
cheese illustrates its image as divine.

It's primitive, though, dating from the stage
when wandering animals became a herd—
yet classical, part of the Golden Age,
idyllic piping and the poets' word.

Thus cheese—fresh, half- or well-aged, overripe—
from cattle, camel, zebu, sheep, goat, yak,
refers us always to its prototype—
refreshment humble or symposiac.

What ingenuity in cheese! How neat, how apt,
according to the circumstance, the beast—
a model of how human beings adapt,
devising, for a common need, a feast.

The more amazingly: it's rotten stuff,
first soured and curdled, pressed, then left to mould—
fulfillment of a gastronomic bluff,
most aromatic, flavorful when old.

It's all a matter, to be sure, of taste.
While one prefers a muscled cheese, strong nerve,
another favors oozing, glaucous paste,
its subtle cream, its delicate reserve.

I fancy toothsome, hard cheese—Emmental,
Comté—or semi-hard—Cantal—or blue:
blue Stilton, gorgonzola, Roquefort, all—
(such blue blood in the veins!); so I eschew

fromage coulant—that runny Camembert,
Maroilles, Neufchâtel, and every Brie;
the crust is awful; chalky white, like glaire,
red rind, or ashen-gray, it sickens me.

The cheese, our handiwork, reflects our state:
endowed like gods, inventive and refined,
but cast in carnal matter by our fate,
strange, odorous, perverse—the taste of mind.

Egret by the Pond

A crank, a busybody—call me what
you wish. I'm not an ornithologist,
nor even active in a bird club—no;
instead, an avian fan. Doves, mockingbirds,
and meadowlarks, jays, phoebes, cardinals,
hawks, canyon wrens—these creatures who gave joy
day-long in western light still flutter, sport,
fly up in memory; and Houston's got

fine waterfowl and waders—herons, ducks,
great egrets. So, this morning, looking out
by chance, I saw a gardener below—
misguided, cruel?—endeavor to drive off
a great white egret striding on the bank
along the bayou. True, it has the nerve
to visit sometimes at our high-rise home—
glide in among the trees, alight, assume

a post beside our pond, stand vigilant,
then spear at goldfish. True, those fish are *ours*,
not his (the egret's). On *my* watch, we'll have
no persecution, though, of birds. The man
first waved his arms and yelled, I think, then ran,
picked up a clod of earth, and hurled it, hard.
The bird had flown off, well before, and crossed
the bayou, but returned, with wing-control

amazing, a delight. The workman, vexed,
attempted to pursue the egret, threw
another clod—in vain, of course. By now,
irate, I'd reached the hall, was soon downstairs
and out, complaint all formulated. Few,
perhaps, will understand such urgency
for just a bird. From nests in Hermann Park,
new eggs will give new birds, as nature sees

continuously to survival; what,
however fine he is, can one bird mean?
It's nothing: only beauty on the wing—
fantastic, feathered rhapsody of flight,
both alien dream and real, as real as flesh—
which lifts me like an Icarus, but safe,
our vulnerable bodies joined to soar—
frail majesty, unfettered though, alive.

Bluebonnets

—For Tom and Nancy Eubank

Alone, they're diffident, almost withdrawn—
a modest flower in a garden bed,
two little plants mown level with a lawn,
low-profiled, barely hanging on. But spread

in copious ranks of blossoms by the road
or, tens of millions, crossing fields, abreast,
they turn the earth to blue, a mother lode
of pure cerulean sensation, pressed

into a memory. What lovely chance
that they are here, and *we!*—conjunctions rare
of matter in the universal dance:
raw gaseous stuff made joyful and aware,

like us; or formed in leaf and lazuline—
innumerable facts of chlorophyll,
soil, water, sunlight, miracle of green.
Blue cohorts are arrayed on every hill

now, rising to the crests and azure skies
astir with spring—the airy counterpart
of earth's display, reflected in your eyes,
deep microcosm of vast cosmic art.

Carrots

A bunch of carrots on the cutting board
have caught the corner of my eye with strange,
self-designating presence. Might they be
five virgins waiting to be sacrificed?
Plump fingers, reddened, puffy from the gout?
Mute nobles lined up for the guillotine?
Or are they, rather, mermaids, bodies slim
and tapered to a point, with leafy hair—

Ophelia's locks, or delicate green strands
in the Sargasso Sea? I do not like
the thought of immolating even flesh
imagined; so I'll think of them as stuff,
just vegetable matter, crisp and hard,
resistant to the knife, a test for teeth.
The tops go first: a quick beheading. Next,
the skin: I take the peeler, scrape away.

"Dice carrots finely," says the recipe.
But what's to keep them rolling from the board?
Bisecting them is tricky; then the halves
must be cut up, and so on, till the bits
are flying to all sides, and meanwhile I
am fearful for my fingers, even eyes.
All this for plain beef stew! I'm not a cook,
or barely; less, a surgeon, seamstress, tooth-

extractor with strong hands. Two fragments fall
beneath the table, others down a crack
beside the stove. Farewell. —A friend once said
I didn't seem to care for food. Not so;
the best meals, though, are cooked by someone else,
and, preferably, Texas-style, robust,
with little snobbery. —Back to the board.
Ah well; at least there is no blood to stanch,

and now the orange gems are in the pot,
contributing their color, vitamins,
and taste (if it survives long hours
of heat). Ah, vegetables! Children's bane,
but comfort to the conscience, a relief
from guilty flesh—since from mere cellulose,
insentient, we concoct its opposite,
brilliant conceit of nothingness, of joy.

Sparrows

—For David and Lesley Walker

In a Yorkshire winter, as I walked down from Broomhill
past shops, banks, pubs, and football pitches
to the museum and the university,
I'd watch the little birds flitting in the barren trees
and shrubbery, pecking through snow
in gardens, scavenging for crumbs along the walkway
by a pastry shop. I'd step into the park to take
the back way toward the Arts Tower and meander

among the statuesque but leafless trees, which looked
as frozen as I felt—shivering despite beret, gloves,
woolen scarf, and heavy overcoat,
bought in Chicago. The sparrows would dart out,
as if to greet me, from the limbs and thickets,
tap at patches where the snow had melted or had blown
away, flutter upwards then—wingèd seeds cast
by a sower's hand. Traffic noises faded. Were the birds

as glad as I to have a respite, if not from the cold, at least
from din of lorries, taxis, busses shifting, grinding
through the slush? To me, the little creatures
were companions, like Silvio Pellico's spider,
which he trained to eat out of his hand
in his prison cell—and which the jailers killed, I think.
For avian company, I still am grateful now,
as for all those whose presence blossomed for me—tulips,

→

61

daffodils in March, bright roses later. And here beside me
on the desk is posed a token of that courtesy,
those ties: a common house sparrow—such an English
bird!—in Royal Crown Derby, given
to us for our marriage by dear Yorkshire friends
when we dined there in a seafood bistro last November—
rain in our collars earlier, and bitter wind, but bands
of sparrows offering feathered welcome, flights of memory.

Trees in a Park

—For Peter and Margot Fawcett

Above the desk, a gift from English friends—
fine trees, artistically photographed
on textured paper, framed and matted—lends
its shady pleasure to our room. A shaft

of sunlight, painterly, allows the eyes
to glimpse a clearing with a statue, nude,
well-suited to a satyr's enterprise,
inviting wood nymphs' games and lyric mood.

The foliage varies—almost pale to dark,
boughs lateral or bending, canopied;
the trunks are slightly slanted, and the bark
brown, blackish, grey, according to its creed.

These specimens provide a paradigm
of form and function realized in green,
proposing branches, leaves, soft grass as time
arboreal, reflected and serene.

Imagining a leafy, forest feel,
I let my gaze stroll leisurely, at ease,
to verify in nature the ideal,
and know why lovers often favor trees.

III: The Scripted Fate

Sarabande

This stately piece by Handel was a staple
of my childhood keyboard practice. Here are annotations
in the hand of my aunt Mary—my sole teacher—
to improve the fingering proposed and indicate
new phrasing. We did not have an instrument
ourselves, except, for brief years, the Brambach baby grand
belonging to another aunt—which, rebuilt,
refinished, tuned, following Katrina's damp misdeeds,

occupies this room. My father played by ear, and well;
but he depended, as I did, on pianos elsewhere—
Aunt Mary's Steinway at my grandparents', the Brambach,
another Steinway at his brother's house.
"Wash your hands before you touch the keys!"
Aunt Mary cautioned me. Fair enough, given
that I was a tomboy, outdoors more than in.
She showed great patience.—Once, my grandmother,

considerate and generous, ordered (a surprise gift
for my father) a good upright, secondhand.
It was delivered, somewhat dirty. I came home from school
to find my mother, furious, telling him
it could not be accepted, covered as it was with dust.
A pretext? Anyhow, it was refused. That day, her love
for both of us failed greatly. For some years,
the subject of pianos was not raised. I practiced

→

at the aunts', worked through students' books, learned
four-part pieces, sang. Handel stayed
with me, my fingers keeping somehow its broad measures
and its sonorous bass line, moving evenly
under the treble chords. Though in a minor key,
it speaks serenely now, the way a placid statue
emerges from rough stone—disharmonies
and old missteps yielding to the ordered dance of age.

Del Rio & Winter Garden

Given that I'm speaking of the Big Bend in West Texas,
near the Davis Mountains—high desert,
rocky, barren, often raw in wintertime, never much
like Eden, not even at the lower altitudes
along the Rio Grande—"Winter Garden" was a misnomer;
still, it was that small outfit from Del Rio, 200 miles
downriver, that provided us with telephones
and telegraph at mid-century, connecting us—along

with mail, radio, Southern Pacific trains—to each other
and parts of the world. My father's restlessness
had taken us to that spare land. Twice before, we'd set out
from Colorado: once for Arizona,
later for South Texas, which turned out to be
too damp, unhealthy. This time we'd broken ties for good,
in mid-October—his post resigned, school
interrupted, house on the market, maps spread out:

New Mexico and Texas. He'd wanted winter sun (if cold)
but, even more, dry air for his lungs, simplicity
of life, and isolation, free from crowds.
I did not mind uprooting; though I loved and needed
mountains, girlhood was in me, not in the world.
And what my father did was well done, always. That
was his gift, and my inheritance—not slight.
We stopped beside the Pecos River crossing, I remember,

where he took a photo of me—cowboy shirt, boy's jeans;
we saw the springs at Balmorhea, a startling oasis.
On the road, mirages pooled; and how the mountains shone
in the clear turquoise of a West Texas autumn!—
an upland hermitage, and not a wilderness.
We found a one-room college cottage, since destroyed;
my mother, stronger, got a job. We had no phone
for months, managing with letters to the Colorado family,

knowing no one else to call, anyway. At last, a few
friends, a bargain house, and that umbilical attachment
by which, later, Father learned that Grandmother
was dying. Our number then was 394B—a party line,
rarely used at first; but when I was sixteen
it proved an honorable means of being courted. That mode
of life seems distant now, and might be judged
archaic, simpleminded, marked by poverty of vision;

there, no one traveled round the globe, got the *cordon
bleu*, or made millions; few made much at all.
My father planted trees, well-watered—tall now, leafy,
according to a friend's photograph. I wish
I could embrace them, or devise a wire connecting me
to what is past. In the cemetery, cypress sway above
parched grass, shading the sunken graves;
dust devils—desert genies—dance and stir the endless sand.

Blue Norther

We used to watch blue northers blowing down
from the Glass and Davis Mountains,
occupying in the distance the full theater of sky,
with rain cascading hard in a dark scrim
behind the proscenium arch. Then,
as in courtyard drama, the vanguard edge of cloud—
its outline inked in strokes of black
and Prussian blue—would advance toward us,

pushing aside the warmer air and hanging almost
motionless, it seemed, its underside
exposed and caught along the ramparts and rocky
palisades that overlook the rangeland. A few
ragged threads would dangle from the laden
mass as the front ranks stormed ahead,
baring their teeth.—This afternoon, we've come
out, happy, to our balcony, with perfect sunshine, sky

the hue of robin's egg, adorned by only cirrus
feathers and one great egret gliding
calmly to the bayou. But yesterday, commotion
reached us from the Panhandle, besieging
Houston with all its theatrical machinery—
curtains of rain, lightning exchanging charges,
thunder blustering, and clouds the blue
of angry waters, or mad eyes. It's *déjà vu*, the best

→

and worst together.—Demons will be with me
always, I believe—childhood apprehensions
lurking, dancing, eddying—marsh deities cavorting
in the darkness, flashing false light, or perhaps
real conflagrations. It is not enough
to say "How fortunate I am!"—books, music,
family, friends, and, foremost, love. Look
at Steiner in *La Dolce Vita!* One must exorcise, yes,

exorcise! "Oh, the horror of it all!" Where are
my parents now, who watched the storm with me?
Dead, of course, but that's just pushing back
the question. Mexicans still celebrate
El Día de los Muertos by eating sugar skulls,
decorating graves, and carrying dark-eyed skeletons
in the streets, or visiting the mummies
on velvet cushions in the catacombs of Guanajuato,

"Hill of Frogs." Somehow, demons must be changed
to *daemons*, those attendant spirits or powers
who guide us better than ourselves. It's Halloween:
high above the city's scenery, a small plane
pulls a sign advertising "Houston Haunted House."
But I have ghosts enough; I'd prefer
herald winds, a dark assault of nimbostratus
cloud, memories: the words "Blue Norther on the Way."

For a Late Cat (I)

He lived for thirteen years and saw with me,
his restless friend, eight states by road.
A furry waif without a pedigree,
found in a nearby street, he owed

his welfare to benevolence of fate,
and to a neighbor's clever act,
when she recalled my solitary state.
It was, though, really *I,* in fact,

who was more favored. He had beauty, wit,
good feline character; he brought,
by simply *being,* joy and benefit.
Though watched and cherished, he was caught

at last within mortality's vast net,
to feed its awful appetite.
I cannot say how deeply I regret
your death, sweet Dill. *Vale,* good night.

For a Late Cat (II)

Last year, at a New Mexico motel—
attractive pueblo styling and decor—
we settled in, the cat included—well,
we thought. At ease, he started to explore

a table with a forged-iron lamp. Somehow,
his leash (still on for safety) got entangled
among volutes. He turned, was caught. The row
was terrifying: he was nearly strangled

as he pulled, then tried to run, then leapt,
or fell, with lampshade, lamp, and cord attached.
He howled and snarled, he hissed, he jerked. I kept
my senses, lunged for him, but missed—ill-matched,

since *he* was frenzied, crazed, *I* just concerned.
The shade encumbered us; the bulb, still hot,
rolled round with him; I feared he would be burned.
I caught him finally, undid a knot

that nearly choked him, shook him free, and got
him, trembling, to the bed. His gorgeous eyes—
green, jungle-bright—were wild with fear, but not
resentment: a disquieting surprise

was not malign intention on my part,
he knew.—Such trust! And did the universe
seem beneficent to his feline heart?
Or did he feel, as we, the fatal curse

of being—lamps malicious, mortal rope?
At last, the leash of time around his neck
was drawn too tight; however I might hope,
love could not save him from life's final wreck.

Evelyn

How could we not be friends? —a subtle bond,
distinguished, firm: steel cable, silken thread.
Imagine Texas at mid-century;
hot desert winds, an isolated town,
the dog days, two girls meeting. She appeared
one afternoon, accompanied of course
by parents, who had chosen to drive far
to meet the family of the girl who'd be

her college housemate. As the visit sped,
we took each other's measure, youthfully.
Each was reserved (it was our character;
it was the time), devoted, almost grave
in learning, snobs in poetry and art—
iron filings similarly magnetized—
eschewing all rebellion and pretense.
The friendship lasted nearly fifty years,

did me great honor, lent me other eyes.
No one assented more to what I was,
nor read me so astutely; I became
(she was not bold, nor well) her daring self,
her bosom's vagabond, her risk. What cares
she had were quiet—love for husband, son,
a few well-chosen causes, and the mind's
fine cultivation. Evelyn, I miss

our conversations—bright and lively flames,
low embers that we fanned a later day
or year to start all over—as I miss
your letters, mirrors of your lucid thought,
where judgment governed—sunbeams through the motes
of true and false—illuminating all
by words well-chosen, giving voice to what
we felt that summer, stepping into life.

For Friends of a Man
Who Died in a Las Vegas Casino

A recent widower, not well, he flew
to Vegas with his son—an escapade
postponed for years. It was a rendezvous,
his last, with fortune: every hand he played

(he did not know) was also an adieu—
a final toast to luck, a debt he weighed
and settled—an ironic, wry review
of odds, before life's ultimate charade.

He briefly lost, then magnetized the cards,
amazed and grateful. When he drew a straight,
he quit, and changed his chips for dollars—shards

and tokens of success.—Believe in Fate,
which reckons by its own arithmetic:
he fell and died, a fitting end, and quick.

To a Friend Whose Husband Died
in the Madrid Airport

He might have planned and written out the script:
death took him unawares, just off the plane,
en route with you to Venice. Something tripped
a switch in him then; he could not refrain

from moaning slightly. Pale, you said, he gripped
a handrail as he pulled his case. Urbane
though, always, he sat down, then gasped, and slipped
into long sleep without a sign of pain.

What smoother way to leave, how fit the date—
at Christmastide, while stopping in Madrid—
for one at home by a departure gate,

who thrived on foreign travel as he did!
However we love life, death loves us more.
They've flown together to a distant shore.

For a Friend Grieving
After an Unexpected Death

Rota fortuna turns; you've often found
yourself descending in the darkness—chance
deceiving you. This year, the thread unwound
again, a sudden fall, by circumstance

and routine surgery. —He was your ground,
your hold on things. He struggled, but the dance
of death had started in its chilling round
and drew him on, a mocking of romance;

and as a full man, ponderous, he gave
uncommon purchase to the scythe. —The bird
of mind has flown; the flesh is in the grave.

What killed him was, apparently, his heart.
How love sustains us, breaks us, with a word!
—in life, and death, the body's counterpart.

For One Whose Husband Drowned
in the Backyard Pool

Fate's appetite, like beauty, is a ghoul.
Picture a man, still sturdy in his way,
who undertakes to clean the backyard pool,
and drowns. —Late afternoon, a sultry day,

without relief, except the water, cool.
Leaves gone, he frolics, swims, and tosses spray
with sower's gestures, languidly—death's fool,
as are we all.—It's time for Tanqueray,

vermouth, crushed ice, and rest.—Imagine how,
at ease, you steer your float; you take a drink;
you pull your hat brim down, and barely blink,

as sunlight ebbs and sleep encroaches. Now,
you sleep forever. We are happenstance,
blue figures leaning in a liquid dance.

To a Close Friend
Whose Father Hanged Himself

How did you face his death, self-willed and raw?
You have endured it since that day you found
him in the cellar, dangling in the maw
of nothingness, past purchase, without ground.

Mortality had stalked him: heavy paw
on shoulder, breath an eager heat around
his heart. Advancing, he embraced its law—
God-fearing, yet confronting heaven's hound,

or hell's. In time, you tried to reproduce
that anguish and resolve, make them your own—
memorial, or catharsis of the noose—

so that in death he should not be alone.
You tell me you and grief have signed a truce.—
Tears, seeping, shine, as from a river stone.

Edith's Party

No one knows how many people gathered
for the great occasion, Edith's natal celebration,
which should have been in January
but, like the Queen's, had been postponed till June
for better weather (this is Colorado). I
am Edith's cousin-german; her sister came, of course,
with husband, their four children
(two spouses also) and six grandchildren (of nine).

There were two of Edith's husband's offspring,
accompanied, and nieces and four nephews (children
of her brother John) from Illinois
and South Carolina. Father Mike, the local priest,
was there; her husband's brother's widow,
also, down from the Grand Mesa. Near neighbors—
six at least—dropped in, and two old women
from a seniors' colony; others whom I don't recall

and thus can't count. The rowdy dogs, though,
can be numbered—seven!—mostly hunting dogs,
all in the house at once because of rain,
a rare treat from the gods where summer clouds
are bluster, usually. Not that the canines
care; but someone wants to keep them dry. Outside,
everything is wet: the lawn, the pergola,
where serving tables are set up, a rented tent, hard-

buffeted by wind, the aspen trees, which shake
themselves just like the dogs, now out
(the rain has ended), romping, leaping,
chasing each other, bathing in the ornamental pool.
A patch of blue appears. In the kitchen,
half a dozen cooks and helpers struggle. Well,
they don't need me. In the solar room, I find a bit
of quiet and look westward toward the "Monument,"

that massive tide of stone which breaks and taluses
onto the sand. "Lo! what a cloud of witnesses
encompass us around"—the ruddy lithic
evidence of earth a hundred million years ago,
some two-score visitors today, the dogs, perhaps
even the dead, now smiling at us
like the sun—remembering a blond-haired girl
at play, and musing, taking a long, long view on life.

The Eagle

The hostess in that Montmartre night club—filled
with Americans, I think, that summer (sixty-two),
as well as French, Brits, Germans—had her routine:
she'd go around the tables with a pair of scissors,
telling men to sing, or she'd cut off their neckties.
Few obliged—and thus she snipped, to laughter.
In those years, Pat wore bow ties. She could have
clipped the corners, I suppose. No need: Pat sings

with vigor and knows scores of songs—American
and Irish; he's not reticent. At my request, he did
"I'll Take You Home Again, Kathleen." Not all,
of course, could catch the words. They could not
miss the man, however—gorgeous tenor, dark-blue
suit (travelers dressed well, then), fine form. It was
our final summer as young lovers, married, happy.
What good prospects lay ahead!—We flew back

separately though, to different coasts, and lived apart
until we grew too distant. Afterwards, I could not
hear "Kathleen" or even think of it without remorse
and misery—the stinging kind that makes you strike
out in your mind, sometimes in body, at yourself.
My thoughts would leap to California, as I yearned
for home, for anywhere again with him—recalling,
while I wept, our Paris holiday, its promises forever

→

broken. My own doing. I gnawed long at my heart.
Who needs an eagle? Chained, Prometheus had his,
but he was a Titan; we are merely human. So we are
our own tormentors. Even now, surrounded—after
our remarriage—by Pat's loving, I can be devoured
with regrets when memory strikes, jarred by a book,
a name—dry lightning without rain; no tears, though,
only Furies, hissing, dressed in tatters of the past.

On Seeing Patric Again

He'd changed, of course, although not greatly—just
less trim, lined brow, deep marks around his eyes
and mouth, hair silvered, thinning, as it must—
aged, altered, but still Pat, without surprise.

Was I, though altered, likewise yet myself,
according to some inner law—new name,
old girl—a novel yellowed on the shelf,
its binding worn, its heroine the same?

No matter: in a lengthy, sweet embrace,
tight evidence of old love newly-found,
we recognized, each on the other's face,
the person of the past, gone underground.

Now, peeling off disguise, and mocking age,
we know each other not as each appears,
but by the four dimensions of love's gauge—
two bodies, and the imprint of long years.

Growing Pains

Take the phrase as you wish—we've nearly all
experienced growing pains in childhood:
legs tingling, strangely occupied
as if by wigglers; arms uneasy in the bed;
or, metaphorically, the harsh discovery
that the world is alien and may not bend to will
and action—or may yield, at best,
on its terms only. "The moon, the moon—

I want the moon. That's all." And thus Caligula,
in Camus's play, expressed his wish
for mastery and being, absolute. And *he*
was emperor! But that was not enough—
imagination and desire are vaster
than an empire.—The feeling is still worse
a few years later, when you wrestle
with the angel who announces your adulthood,

and the givens of your situation are quite clear,
but you cannot consent yet to make peace
with them.—Now Pat, aged eighty,
has new growing pains! Not the existential sort,
of course, but sharp pains in his leg,
where nerves are trying to come back
after a surgeon opened at the shinbone
a broad triangle, peeled back the skin, and then

removed a piece of flesh the size of a large olive.
What was left was just a cavity
with sutures at the sides; and now the leg
is trying mightily to mend itself.
It's possible: we mended broken love,
hearts wiser, more devoted than before,
the early hurts repaired. Your leg will heal;
we'll stride together, reconciled, needing no moon.

Abed

The current Queen and I are of one mind,
at least concerning bedclothes. I'll explain.
We don't like comforters (the bulky kind),
duvets, or quilts. The heavy counterpane

a posh hotel may boast must be removed
for royal stay. *I* can't demand the same,
with no authority, alas (that's proved),
possessing nothing like the monarch's fame—

but in my private life and private bed,
I can pursue my own neurotic war.
At night, I carefully roll up the spread
(Pat's eiderdown) and place it on the floor,

exposing pleasing textures—cotton sheet
in summer for a dreamer's drowsy sail;
in winter, wool. A duvet can't compete—
synthetic fabrics are of small avail,

and goose down, although light, must yield to sheep's
superior genius. On the soft expanse
of blanket, arms are stretched. Before he sleeps,
Pat holds my hand. We doze; our fingers dance;

I feel the blanket and admire the weave,
the thickness—insulation without weight—
and think of mountain meadows, the naive
endowment of the flocks, nature's estate.

Abed in love's ideal *Gemütlichkeit*,
the covers close, or partly folded back,
but shaped well to our bodies for the night—
a reassuring, warming cul-de-sac—

we settle in each other's arms and praise
the elements of tardy happiness:
sweet intimacy in the dark; fair days;
the loom of fate; high grazing lands' largesse.

An Evening at Eleanor's

—For Eleanor and Roger Beebe

Kirs before dinner, in honor of our dead friend Mary Ann,
who lived in France, and of Patricia, here from Austin—
though some don't drink (the pregnant wife
of Eleanor and Roger's son, and Pat, whose cardiologist
forbids it). Then delicious food, low-cal, in honor
of our age (for the AARP-eligible five, both cancers
and heart surgeries; this is the rehabilitation ward,
so to speak). Afterwards, champagne. Mark (the son)

and Pat sing silly songs; Pat plays a "Gnossienne" by Satie.
We reminisce, of course—four of us go back quite far—
remembering an evening when we dined
with Gabriel Marcel, after he'd lectured earlier that day
at Rice. The great man, gentle, gracious, who denied
having a philosophy (perhaps the best variety
of thinker), spoke of the concrete, immediate; of *being*
and its mystery. Young then—the eldest just past thirty—

we were caught up in our existence, at the prow of action—
speedboats leaping through the water's dark
resistance, bright aerolites of possibility,
phosphorescence in the heavens' surf. Those trajectories
are traced now—weddings, children, travels,
a divorce or so, careers, and deaths. We can no longer
borrow the heady talk of black-clad '50s denizens
of the Left Bank, nor be so self-assured; we're quieter

and deal more in the mode of Marcel's searching dialogue,
thinking *être*, not *faire* or *avoir*, taking ebullience
in little doses only, treasuring each other's
being—barrier islands against the sea, mysterious, dark,
the contours of existence shaped behind us.
The net was cast far out, but now the tides have drawn
it in. It's late; we seven say goodnight,
under a full moon riding the zenith, and great reefs of stars.

Anniversary

—Cascade, Colorado, July 2010

Our second anniversary today—
our second marriage! Thus we celebrate
this windfall happiness in its own way,
reliving weddings and disunion on one date.

Perhaps the fates selected us quite young—
ambitious, talented, attracting light
but also fire—to have us thrown among
uncertain prospects, beasts with appetite.

The fault cannot be others', though; assured
of love, we should have tended well both heart
and mind; but somehow we became unmoored,
as omens gathered, dark birds, at the start.

Remember how a clergyman declined
(some petty matter)—though all was arranged—
to marry us? What virtue could he find
in such an ostentatious act? We changed

the printed cards—a new time and address.
That church was later razed—disuse,
greed of developers, divine distress?
The past is moot. By now we've signed a truce

not only with ourselves, but the decree
that separated us, which we have burned,
and intervening years—while destiny,
indulgent or appeased by age, has turned

a favorable face. Around the Peak,
the wind is stirring, fresh, in many voices;
together, we are dyad, concord. Speak,
Erato; memory at last rejoices.

IV. Themes for the Muses

At the Ballet

A bold conception, said to be first class,
with varied styles of gesture, steps, and play,
plus music, avant-garde, by Philip Glass—
I'm speaking of a Twyla Tharp ballet.

The scoring calls for strings, flute, lots of brass,
and electronic noises. All convey
remarkable monotony, alas.
The chords will not resolve, nor go away;

redundant sound continues to unwind,
progressing, yet immobile, incomplete—
a cruel teasing of the ordered mind—
while, sneaker-clad or slippered, flying feet

and twirling bodies, solo or entwined,
exhaust themselves, obedient to the beat—
a tarantella of the classic kind,
with fiery intensity, yet neat.

The dancers' movements are their very thought,
as muscles and idea impose belief
in will and weightless being, beauty-fraught,
suspended for long moments, madly brief.

At last, the stubborn threads of sound are caught,
ascending in close harmony, a sheaf
of light. Too late: it ends. The music's wrought
its magic; now, time, fleeting, is a thief.

Beaumarchais in the Tribunal

Endowed in every way—audacity,
great ingenuity, good looks, and charm—
Caron de Beaumarchais had talent, too,
for getting into trouble. Not that he
desired it, but difficulties lie
in wait for those who are successful. Spite,
resentment, envy, from aristocrats
and varlets both, pursued him; women loved

him wildly and were jealous; one mad duke,
enraged because his mistress had gone off
and left him for the playwright, tried to kill
him in his own salon. As Beaumarchais
ran many hares at once, he was accused
of poaching, so to speak, and found himself
among the hunted then. A popinjay,
whose uncle had been kind to Beaumarchais

and left him money, sued him in the courts,
accusing him of forgery and theft.
The custom then was to solicit those
connected to one's case—"assessor," judge.
The Barber of Seville, meanwhile, was due
to open in a fortnight; anxious crowds
already knew the story. Suddenly,
rehearsals ceased; the author was in jail,

by royal *lettre de cachet!* The duke
(who'd "troubled to be born and nothing else")
was locked up elsewhere; Beaumarchais must go.
So from a cell in For-l'Evêque, the man
who had created Figaro set out
to fight the king's decree and influence
those who would judge him in the popinjay's
complaint. To visit someone, you must first

be free. He wrote and wrote, in vain; his tone
was not subservient. At last, a friend
advised him to show penitence and beg.
To beg, for Figaro! Still, pride's a dish
that must be often sacrificed for meats
of substance. Prostrate, he admitted wrong,
implored the privilege to spend some hours—
as other prisoners did—outside the walls,

and finally was allowed to leave, with guards,
to plead his case. The court assessor's wife,
he learned, would look with favor on a gift;
two hundred *louis* passed into her hands.
But that was not enough. A diamond watch—
a jewel of the playwright's early skill—
was added, and an attaché was bribed.
Alas, the adversary had prevailed

already, by still greater gifts; the court
found Beaumarchais at fault, assessed a fine
—almost three thousand *louis d'or* plus costs—
and seized his properties. Outraged, he asked
that all the bribes, at least, be given back.
He got the watch, the *louis d'or*, but not
the final gift. It was his chance. Released
from prison after weeks, he spread the word

→

that an assessor's wife had taken bribes.
A bold move, worthy of his Figaro—
a gamble also: bringing justice down,
he might bring down himself as well.
Obliged to counter, the assessor found
a witness to suborn, then filed complaints
against poor Beaumarchais for calumny.
No lawyer dared to take his case; he pled

his own. All Paris watched and talked; gazettes
and gossip thrived. He wrote four legal briefs
and published them. Such a defense! His aim
was to intrigue the public—move, impassion,
and amuse it, as he did with *Figaro*—
in service of the truth. He spared no barb,
no wit, no revelation. "What a man!"—
so wrote Voltaire to d'Alembert. The king

(quite tolerant) and Madame du Barry
dissolved in laughter, reading. What would count,
though, was the playwright's day in court. It came.
The perjured witness, fearing Heaven, renounced
his statement; Beaumarchais, who learned the facts
by chance, revealed his enemy had left
without resource a child of his, produced
by an illicit liaison. Was this

the sort of magistrate desired, a man
who had neglected his own child, whose wife
had taken gold for him and then purloined
some? The performance was a triumph; truth
was out. A greater play, the *Barber*, took
its place upon the boards; beyond, alas,
lay history's bloody turmoil—not the light
men needed, but the guillotine's black stage.

In the Brooklyn Museum

Classic architecture facing us—pillars, pediment, and dome,
the image of imposing, institutionalized art;
but here's a new glass entrance hall, skylit, feeling open,
vast—and, greeting us, more living than the bag inspector,
are twelve Rodin statues, not life-sized
but enormous, giants of his thought. He cast them extra-
large because the early critics had alleged
his "Le Vaincu" had been molded from a living model—

unacceptable technique; the statue was too good (the pose,
the lifted arms showing the biceps,
the mighty neck and rippling torso, musculature in bronze,
almost breathing). Here's Balzac, naked,
corpulent, and vigorous—the vision of the *Comédie humaine*
in person; here, too, the tragic burghers of Calais,
standing alone, the more impressive for it
(hands enormous, palpitant; feet, the very sense of motion,

fit for a colossus; heads, even in their lamentation, strong):
Andrieus d'Andres, the "weeping burgher,"
fingers enmeshed, covering his head in dolor; Jean d'Aire,
holding the city key to be surrendered;
Pierre de Wiessant—like others, rope around the neck;
two more; finally, Eustache de Saint-Pierre,
the bearded burgher, at the center of the monument of six
erected in Calais. All are immense, with eyes far-seeing

→

in their sacrifice, proclaiming still their fear of martyrdom,
their grief, their pride. The massive presences
confound all critics, as they challenge matter, using
earth in common species—tin and copper ores—fire, and air,
to go beyond it, to surpass the suffering body,
hostage to history—not just the forlorn burghers of Calais,
but vulnerable France, occupied by English
hundreds of years, vanquished on the fields of Waterloo,

once again defeated at Sedan in 1870, amputated of Alsace,
Lorraine. Did Rodin also think of women's bodies—
fragile rose and pale-gold flesh destroyed—
like those he loved (too well), preserved in his erotic sketches?
—We have had enough for now; we round up children,
move into the main pavilion, get our tickets,
visit the European paintings, arranged by genre in a square
so that portraits on one side stare at our backs as we admire

the landscapes opposite. Then luncheon. But Rodin cannot
be ignored; going out, we stop once more,
marvel, watch the children run among the statues, laughing,
small limbs lively, full of future, friable
though, destined to dissolve in time—even as they resist idea,
the pure bronze of the mind, transcending
such imagined pathos in their midst—art and being in pursuit
of one another, shadows leapfrogging, wrestling in the grass.

Liszt in Weimar

The Grand Duke was responsible, to start,
inviting Liszt to Weimar for three months
each year to serve him in a special post
as Kapellmeister *extraordinaire*.
It was mid-century, or nearly—soon the time
of revolution, turmoil in the air,
wild aspirations among peoples, hopes
for new republics, tyranny dissolved.

Already, Weimar was a beacon—Bach,
then Goethe, Wieland, Schiller, all had lived
there; Duke Carl August had established rule
by constitution, and his son would keep
disorder from the streets. In 'forty-eight
Liszt left the concert tour—a master still,
phenomenal—and took up residence.
The greater honor was the duke's. Liszt's friends,

drawn by his magnet, visited or sent
their music for performance. And what friends!
Von Bülow, Wagner, Schumann, Berlioz,
and others. The premier of *Lohengrin*
was due to him; of Schumann's *Manfred* too;
and Liszt composed frenetically new works,
then played them or conducted. Heady times,
those were. As he had gone around the world

→

of concert halls before, the world now came
to him. A woman friend had joined him—just,
he thought, to spend a fortnight, planning next
to take the waters. Having left her vast estate
in Russia, Carolyne Sayn-Wittgenstein
arrived to stay, however—lover, muse,
amanuensis, confidante. Thenceforth
for thirteen years they lived as one. To wed,

though, was not possible: Marie d'Agoult—
the mother of Liszt's children—never was
his wife; thus he was free; but Carolyne
was married to a minor prince who loved
her properties and had the Czar's support
and ear. The liaison became at last
notorious. Oddly devout, half-crazed,
she sought annulment, while Liszt's genius,

well complemented by great energy—
an engine running on itself—pursued
its paths, emitting trails of sparks, bright stars
in music's firmament. She left for Rome;
he stayed in Weimar for another year,
but caught misfortune's eye: his grandson died;
in *Das Echo* a vile attack appeared,
approved by Clara Schumann and by Brahms;

the duke turned cool. Near fifty then, but worn,
Liszt went to Paris, made the rounds, performed
before such listeners as Wagner, Berlioz,
Napoleon the Third—saw Delacroix,
met Gounod, offered help to Baudelaire.
Again in Weimar, feted by three days
of valedictories and concerts, Liszt
bade his farewell and left for Italy,

the marriage, wrote Carolyne, arranged
at last. The vows, it seems, would be pronounced
the morning of his birthday, and the church—
the legend says—had been adorned with flowers.
The couple took communion on the eve
of the event. Near midnight, though, a knock
was heard, and Carolyne, in nightdress, learned
the dreadful news: objections being made,

the pope must reconsider everything.
The drama done, she did not try again.
Her hope, which had flamed brilliantly, burnt out—
perhaps quite fake: scenarios of love,
delusions, or a scheme that she devised,
half toying with the future, half deceived,
to satisfy her soul, yet let her play
at holding genius by a wedding band.

In an English Cathedral

Recumbent effigies we can't disturb,
these sleepers, formed of gilded bronze or stone,
are, even in their death, intent, superb—
together joined; together, though, alone.

A king, his robes arranged in careful folds,
his long hair wavy and his eyelids closed,
is guarded by an angel. One hand holds
his shield. Beside him, similarly posed,

with gentler features, lies his handsome queen,
in caul-like headdress, dreamy, hands in prayer.
They yield enormous being—dense, serene—
while absence hangs in the sepulchral air.

Gone, centuries ago, the monarch's rod,
the rivalries and crown of dread, the whirl
of power! Now the armor is for God,
strife having ceased in shroud and marble curl.

—Last night, we lay together on a bed
of love, in quiet ecstasy. No thought
distracted me from you. I stroked your head;
you turned toward me, said something low, and caught

my hand, as if anticipating pain—
not yet, not yet, though.—In descending gloom,
we stroll among our fellows here, who reign
in nothingness. Love is our final room.

Yeats and Maud Gonne, 1891

"To be a poet, first you have to be
a man." So (wisely) said John Butler Yeats
to William. Though we know, in common terms,
what manhood means, the father must have seen,
along with William's gifts, some special need,
some trap, both fallibility and strength.
So William set about the tasks of art
and life together, to become the man

that poetry might honor. Circumstance
was in his favor: Ireland, its pride,
its bondage, all exceptional—a drug,
both stimulant and poison. Then came Maud—
not unconnected in her loveliness,
her energy, to visions of the land
Yeats labored for. In eighteen ninety-one,
when he had dreamed (once more) of her, he left

Orange Ulster and, in Dublin, begged that she
would marry him. She drew her hand away
and said that she would never wed. They spent
the whole next day upon the cliffs at Howth,
beside the Baily lighthouse and the sea.
"Pallas Athene"—so he thought of her.
She went to Paris to resume her work
on Ireland's behalf, but shortly wrote

→

a wrenching letter of wild grief: a child
had died, despite her care, its death announced
by pecking at the window, ominous,
of some dark bird. She sailed for Dublin soon,
returning on the very ship that bore
the body of Parnell. She was in black—
insignia of mourning for the child;
but people thought it was Parnell whose death

she marked, and she was called theatrical.
Yeats met her at the dock; they breakfasted.
She drugged herself to sleep, she said,
by chloroform; she could no longer speak
the French she knew so well. George Russell told
them, later, of clairvoyant means; she asked
when one might be reincarnated, where,
and whether she might hope.—The work of each

continued, fits and starts. Yeats wrote, of course,
those poems of the Irish past. But Maud,
a wounded bird, determined still to flee
his cage, and his proposals were received
predictably. He swore that he would put
his hand into the fire and let it burn,
until she came to recognize his love.
He realized that was madness, though. One night

in France, years later, they made love—a brief
acknowledgment of flesh amid ideals.
He married, finally, another. Words
flowed with abundance, bright or dark, as life
played out—a shadowed figure on the stage,
slim-waisted and fair-haired, who sat, back turned,
at the piano, to play Beethoven;
but when she pivoted, her profile showed,

and then her face—all ravaged, torn by age.
He must, still, love his fate, with whom he danced
long years before, when it had chosen him—
young man, young poet, Ireland, her troth
in body—. . . since, he said, the artist's friend
was Time. He must, thus, let life write
an epitaph, stone-cold, for Sligo. "So,
this is the way it ends; cast your cold eye."

L'elisir d'amore

It's *déjà vu* and *déjà entendu*.
I saw this Donizetti opera
ten years ago, right here, but not with you—
that was before our reconnection. Ah,

I wanted so to glimpse you in the crowd!
Yet what would I have said? Still—half in fear—
I looked around, and nearly spoke aloud
from anxious longing. You did not appear.

Reflecting that Isolde's famous drink
could be effective only in romance,
I bade my friends goodnight. I did not think
the philtre might provide another chance.

It took some seven years, not just a day,
as in the story. Virtue no doubt lies
in yearning; subtle signals may convey
concealed desire and readiness, for eyes

prepared, though unaware. You wrote to me
(thus giving love a cybernetic touch)
to ask about a poet. We agree
you wished for nothing else; and yet so much

ensued, as if a potion in your blood
inspired each to love the other, still.
Your note unlocked in me a weir; the flood
of images came swiftly, as by will.

Now wed, we share in the triumphant bliss
achieved by love's elixir on the stage.
How joyously *amore*'s couples kiss!—
like us: love is the music of our age.

Agnes de Mille in Paris

Her whole life was a gamble, on herself—
her energy and skills, her art, the way
she could imagine dance. America
had not been kind. In Hollywood,
although with family and friends, she found
no audience: producers wanted names
already made, or chorus lines. New York
was not much better—worse, perhaps, since friends

were distant, the expenses great, ballet
the province of the Russians or unknown.
No opera had choreography
(a word still unofficial), and no stage
existed for an innovative style.
She did not merely *think* and *talk* desire;
she danced it—legs, toes, back, arms, hands, and head;
she suffered it, a passion. Thus, she looked

for luck in Paris. Paris! Just the thought—
the Ballets Russes, *Le Sacre du printemps*,
Diaghilev, Nijinsky, and Fokine,
the poetry of flying bodies, feats
of feet. An impresario arranged
her visit, upon payment. Though he was
well-known, he swindled her, an easy fish—
made promises, did little else. She found

the theatre but no publicity,
no management, no help. The stage was spread
with carpet, as impossible for dance as sand.
Linoleum was laid instead; she fell
at the premier—a fine debut. She danced
again, misunderstood, although a friend
stepped up and clapped. Imagination's leaps
in *Danses des plaines de l'ouest* produced

mere bafflement. Where were the gate receipts,
besides? "The tax, Madame; all gone in tax."
Along the Seine and in dim, tiny squares,
she walked in rain among the fallen leaves
and spiky chestnuts, weeping with the skies,
but swore she would get even, or outwit
her fate. Yet she had given in to male
authority so often, "saying yes

but meaning no." Then Brussels was the same:
the small ad called her "Gladys"; not a seat
had yet been sold; the manager presumed
her "Hollywood connections" would take care
of everything when she arrived. Once more,
the audience was cold. In wretched tears,
she took a bow to no applause. Again
in Paris, at the Gare du Nord, she heard

the porter howling for a larger tip.
Farewell to France! Revenge, the proverb says,
can be well eaten cold. Her *Rodeo*,
with Copland's music, ten years later, won
for her a score of curtain calls and fame;
henceforth she danced the west, in flight
as from a bucking horse, and higher still—
for all the world a *Pegasa*, a star.

Stockholm, June 2000

The photos show us in the cocktail bar
of my hotel: a couple—young—and me,
their aging friend, around a table. Far
too many empty bottles for the three

of us. The bartender that summer day,
American, had wanted us to try
a Spanish vintage with a fine bouquet
and body. We were happy to comply.

He then proposed Norwegian aquavit,
expensive, offered gratis—just a taste
remaining in the bottle. Quite a treat
for each, and not a droplet went to waste.

He brought another wine, a good Bordeaux,
to which I'm partial, and a tray of snacks,
the salt of friendship. In the lengthy glow
of northern dusk, we lingered, to relax

and work on appetites. The barman took
our photograph; we finished off the dregs,
put on our jackets, cast a final look,
paid up, and left, on quite unsteady legs,

to find a restaurant nearby. The lights
along the waterfront cast liquid moons,
and frothy stars poured out. Such signal nights
betray us into confidence—dark runes.

Next morning, scanning through *Le Monde*, I read
that "Julius"— my friend Jules Roy, the great—
was gone, aged ninety-two. To know that he was dead
gave retrospectively the feel of fate

to all those hours. "Finis, les longs voyages"
—ascents above the Alps, flights over Spain,
sea crossings, the Sahara's vast mirage,
the heart's wild journeys into love and pain.

Kim Kum-sun

In fifty-eight, five years after the war,
French visitors, the first group from the West,
arrived in Pyongyang to spend five weeks—
a long discovery of North Korea. They
were well received—if absolute control
of movement, contacts, time, and questions posed
(interpreters glued fast), and whirlwind hours
of banquets, speeches, factory tours are viewed

as welcoming. Claude Lanzmann, brave enough
to challenge the routine (a journalist,
he'd fought in the Resistance), feeling sick,
not only of *le monde totalitaire*
around them, but from starving—he could not
endure the dish of honor, "fairies' pot"—
demanded to remain in his hotel
one day, and asked his handlers for a nurse

who might administer a shot of vitamins
(he'd brought with him some phials of B_{12},
almost a cure-all). Kim Kum-sun arrived,
accompanied by half-a-dozen men
in uniform. No words could be exchanged,
since neither knew the other's tongue; she kept
her eyes averted. The next day, she came
again, surrounded. By some ruse, perhaps,

at last she came alone—rouge lips, blue lids,
in Western dress, with "comrade's braids" undone,
her hair cascading down. A sentinel
was posted, mute, but did not interfere.
With passion, Claude and Kim embraced. By signs
and drawings, they agreed to meet at two,
along the river, where a tow path led
toward one of Pyongyang's few pleasures—boats

for rent. He managed to outwit his "guides"
and found her waiting. People stared—they were
conspicuous—but Kim got tickets anyway.
Shoes shed (the rule), toes locked, they got the skiff
into the current. No one was allowed,
however, past a line upstream; a guard
screamed loudly, gestured, threatening. Downstream,
the same restriction; all that one could do

was wander in a circle, fitting form
of a despotic rule. Finally,
they spied a sandbar; in its bend, they moored
and kissed again, with violence, desire
the wilder for its shackles—politics,
no common words, short time, since he would leave
for China soon. As they returned, Kim lost
her balance, toppled, and fell overboard;

she nearly drowned before Claude pulled her out.
Confusion, accusations, reprimands
ensued. He got her, though, to his hotel,
insisted she put on dry clothes—his own—
then walked her out, accompanied again
by uniformed security. She turned
into a doorway, climbed eight flights of stairs,
with him behind, and rang a bell; her look

→

implored him—fear, despair—to leave her there,
renouncing love. He saw her only once
again: a crazed escape from his hotel;
a dash along a road where—miracle
of memory that day—he knew he'd find
the Red Cross hospital; a door; and Kim
a moment in his arms—viaticum
for journeys in the dark. He left a note

with his address, but dared not write from France.
At Christmastime, an envelope arrived—
a postcard picturing a temple, half-
concealed by trees in bloom; on the reverse—
—Korean, with translation—words of peace.
The red lips he remembered seemed to bleed
against the snowy boughs—the wound of love
impossible beneath a scarlet star.

At the Art Show

It's not an ordinary *vernissage*—no stars
or modish gallery, and no *artistes*,
black-clad, bejeweled, of dubious character
and sex, who give "critiques," then mince and laugh
like monkeys. No, this is the tenants' game,
with home-made art, in any mode—pastels,
oils, watercolors, clay, photography,
and even yarn (a shore, blue water, sun).

There's good art, too—a Käthe Kollwitz work,
Chagall (a lithograph)—lent for the show.
Pat's entry is the most unusual,
a hit. In France, in winter 'fifty-four,
on nighttime army duty as a guard
(and it was freezing), he composed a short,
exquisite piece for the piano, called
"Romance." All in his head, of course. He wrote

it down much later, scored it skillfully.
He's had it framed, his personal *objet*,
and then recorded on a CD disk
by a professional. In a recess
a boom-box plays the music; just above,
the framed work hangs. It's synesthesia
and more—calligraphy and symbols, sound
to match the visual referents —and love,

the love imagined in the past for one
unknown, whom he met later, married, lost,
then found again. We stand here, sipping wine,
accepting compliments—though nothing comes
from me, except the distant breath that blew
on embers. New arrivals want to hear
the piece; we listen with them, dark romance
made dazzling in the lingering summer light.

Themes for Piano and Poetry

—after compositions by P.S.

1: Lamentation

It's an ancient theme, lament—not prelapsarian,
but old as exile from the garden, old
as birth and dying, love and war,
connected to them all, with failure, loneliness,
and pain—each wound felt in the heart: that mother
in a legend from Tierra del Fuego,
mourning her dead son: "He was too young to die!";
that prophet—Jeremiah or another—

lamenting lost Jerusalem, the Temple burned,
the Hebrews captive; Antigone,
who grieved over her brother, still unburied;
François Premier, a prisoner—after his enemies
carried the day—wailing aloud, but not
at his own plight—rather, his servant's, borne away
in chains; Milton, Shelley, Tennyson
deploring loss of friends and poets, taken

young. Thus, while modern in its intervals,
your music echoes notes from everywhere, and all
antiquity, as well as this, our misbegotten
century. You sketched it out some fifty years
ago, not knowing what you would lament
in later times—anticipating, though,
inevitable loss. Those chords! You say they mean
an absence: acts undone, and promises

left unfulfilled. Who can measure, finally,
the deeds of man? Yet to dismiss
another's judgment of himself, as though its worth
were doubtful, is to question *him*.
"Oh, the horror of it all!"—time lost,
great gifts distracted, and that sense of emptiness,
the space between the notes, the silence
riffling the air, the heartache when the music ends.

2: Conjecture

Perhaps our whole world is conjecture, supposition,
truth acknowledged but unproven—like
the bold, intuitive idea of Christian Goldbach,
who proposed that even integers of four
or greater were composed of two prime numbers,
and odd integers of three. A game,
now played to astronomical degrees. This music—
written as a tribute, or itself conjecture

in the realm of musical ideas—suggests, not just
between the world—such otherness!—and me,
but in myself, an incommensurable
gulf. Why this, not that? While integers
follow their patterns, *we* are chance,
arranged a bit by choice, compounded with more
chance and variables in dizzying array. What if
my father had not died so suddenly in 1969, leaving

me bereft? Would I have married then? If not,
my daughter would remain unborn, a wish.
Or you could so easily have died,
in '64, with those thromboses—or been paralyzed,
if you'd agreed to one proposal of the doctors.
And so on, until the nose of Cleopatra
shortens, and the battles are not fought, and history
is all rewritten. Such contingency,

expressed in rapid rising and descending phrases,
accidental notes, and most of all that mournful
minor key, natural once, elsewhere
harmonic, with its augmented seventh, bright,
like our finest moments flashing
in a firmament of darkness. So it has been
for me since my fifteenth year. The quarter notes
meet chords in fifths; conjectures settle in the bass.

3: Romance

This too is in a minor key, quite necessarily so
if one considers the trajectories of love.
The music has strange intervals, and, you say, sour
notes, pointed out by question marks
in the notation. But the whole piece is beautiful,
slightly wistful, I suppose, but reminiscent
here and there of Viennese sonorities,
before returning to contemporary modes. What

→

would life be without romance? Did Goldbach love
a woman, once, at least? Love, like music,
clothing, architecture, art, cuisine,
and courtesy, is the redoing or disguise
of immemorial needs or aspirations, most fulfilled
collectively and making us what we call
"human"; art and music are renewed—a stream
of many freshets—and each man, each woman

reinvents the heart. Oh, my beloved! What piece
of music, even by the great Romantics,
or what poem might depict a more extraordinary
feeling than was mine when, after more
than forty years, you wrote that you still loved me?
"Romance," you say, dates from long ago,
and is connected to no sentiment
of yours, but, rather, to the sense of failure

any man will have who loves in vain. But I admire
the brilliant chords, how they exploit,
and then resolve, dissonance—just as, with ease
almost miraculous, we leapt across
long separation—a fire-blue electric arc, singing.
The charge is powerful, casting light
backwards, and creating retrospective harmony—
two staves parallel, lines counterpointed, meeting.

Notes

"Ars poetica." This poem recalls some principles of Horace and of Boileau (1636-1711), the French arbiter of classical prosody. The "streaks of the tulip" is a phrase of Dr. Johnson.

"Six Cold Poems from Colorado." These poems are set mostly in Colorado Springs. The Rampart Range adjoins Pike's Peak.

"North Park." This term refers to a wide, almost flat valley in Jackson County in northern Colorado. There are two similar park-like areas to the south, Middle Park (Grand County) and South Park (Park County).

"Florissant Fossil Beds." This is a National Monument in Teller County, to the west of Colorado Springs and just west of Ute Pass.

"On the Mesa Top." What local residents call "The Monument" is the Colorado National Monument, in far western Colorado, west of Grand Junction. Its stone formations date from the Mesozoic era except for foundational layers and older residue at the canyon bottom. The Monument is mentioned again in "Edith's Party."

"Three for Patric's Eightieth."
"Hibernia." A *ceilidh* is an Irish celebration. Howth is a peninsula, the Eye of Ireland an island. The Deutschen Soldatenfriedhof is a German military cemetery.
"Caledonia." Bridge of Allan adjoins Stirling, northwest of Edinburgh.

"Scarlet Gilia." This plant grows in the Rocky Mountains and westward through what is sometimes called the Sagebrush Steppe. The small trumpet-shaped flowers vary in color from the typical brilliant scarlet to pale pink or yellowish, speckled with red. The habit of picking wildflowers is now discouraged in many areas and banned in national parks and various other locations. In the time, however, of my grandfather (Edward C. Hill, 1863-

1958), when wildflowers were more widespread and human populations much smaller, herbalists and others could collect plants in the wild without fear of depleting the populations. Scarlet gilia, a biennial, even profits from grazing.

"Bluebonnets." This state flower of Texas blooms by the millions in the spring.

"Sparrows." Broomhill is a nineteenth-century suburb of Sheffield. Silvio Pellico (1789-1854), an Italian patriot, was imprisoned by the Austrians for eight years. *My Prisons* relates his experiences.

"Trees in a Park." The photograph described here is by Peter Rawson.

"Del Rio & Winter Garden." The Pecos River crossing mentioned here is in east-central New Mexico.

"Blue Norther." "Oh, the horror of it all" is a notation in "Lamentation," one of three pieces of music by Patric Savage, alluded to in "Themes for Piano and Poetry," the final poems of this collection. In *La Dolce Vita*, Steiner commits suicide, though he has wealth, family, and friends.

"Evelyn." The poem commemorates Evelyn Powell Payne (1935-2001), B.A. Rice Institute, 1956, M.A. Rice, 1963. Her parents lived in Temple, hundreds of miles from my West Texas home.

"On Seeing Patric Again." Readers of *Breakwater* (2009) know that Patric Savage and I met in October 2007 after nearly forty-five years apart and have since remarried.

"Abed." The blanket in question was woven in Routt County, Colorado, of wool from Colorado sheep—hence the allusions to mountain meadows and high grazing lands.

"An Evening at Eleanor's." Gabriel Marcel (1889-1973) was an important French Christian philosopher of the existentialist strain. His major work is *Being and Having*. The image of the speedboat through the water is

128

borrowed not from Marcel but from Jean-Paul Sartre, who used it in connection with the human project, or projection.

"Beaumarchais in the Tribunal." Details of this period in the famous playwright's life come from Maurice Lever, *Beaumarchais*, translated by Susan Emanuel (New York: Farrar, Straus and Giroux, 2009).

"Liszt in Weimar." The information on which this poem is based comes from Derek Watson, *Liszt* (New York: Schirmer Books, 1989).

"Yeats and Maud Gonne, 1891." The information on which this poem is based comes chiefly from Yeats's *Memoirs*, edited by Denis Donoghue (New York: Macmillan, 1972).

"Agnes de Mille in Paris." This poem is based on the dancer's autobiographical volume, *Dance to the Piper* (Boston: Little, Brown, 1952).

"Stockholm, June 2000." The phrase "Finis, les longs voyages" is an echo of *Le Grand Meaulnes* (1913), a much-beloved novel of boyhood wandering, by Alain-Fournier (1886-1914). Jules Roy (1907-2000), born in Algeria, was the premier military novelist of twentieth-century France and, excepting Saint-Exupéry, the finest French writer on aviation.

"Kim Kum-sun." Claude Lanzmann (b. 1925), a journalist (chiefly with *Les Temps Modernes*), is most famous for his film about the Nazi extermination camps, *Shoah*. The information on which this poem is based comes from his memoirs, *Le Lièvre de Patagonie* (2009).

"Themes for Piano and Poetry."
"Conjecture." The conjecture alluded to here, concerning prime numbers, was proposed in 1742 by the Prussian mathematician Christian Goldbach (1690-1764). It was Blaise Pascal (1623–1662) who noted that the history of the world would have been different had Cleopatra's nose been shorter.

5/15/12

811
Bro
Brosman, Catharine Savage

On the North Slope

9/8/12	DATE DUE	
FEB 24 2014		